A Fish Out Of Water

A Christian Perspective on Gender Identity

LINDA HUTCHINS

WestBow Press books may be ordered through booksellers or by contacting:

WestBow Press
A Division of Thomas Nelson & Zondervan
1663 Liberty Drive
Bloomington, IN 47403
www.westbowpress.com
844-714-3454

Scripture taken from the King James Version of the Bible.

ISBN: 978-1-6642-8584-2 (sc)
ISBN: 978-1-6642-8589-7 (hc)
ISBN: 978-1-6642-8587-3 (e)

Library of Congress Control Number: 2022922474

Print information available on the last page.

WestBow Press rev. date: 12/08/2022

WestBow
PRESS®
A DIVISION OF THOMAS NELSON
& ZONDERVAN

Dedicated to my great-grandchildren;
I am thankful that God allowed me
to be a part of their lives.

"For God is not the author of confusion..."
1 Corinthians 14:33

Elliot was a rambunctious five-year-old who loved to play with his unnamed favorite purple puppet. Every time he went to visit his great grandma, Nana, she would let him get the puppet down from the wall hook and play with him. There were other toys to choose from, but the purple puppet was always Elliot's first choice.

This puppet had other puppet friends, but they just didn't capture Elliot's heart the way that the purple one did. The three puppets were special toys that had to be handled very carefully so as not to tangle their strings. Hence, only responsible children could play with them. Therefore, the puppets were not given to the younger children at any time, nor could you get the puppets near the younger children, or they just might get entangled in all the strings.

Nana always reminded the children to be extra careful to keep the puppets out of the reach of the younger kids.

Even when Elliot wasn't at his Nana's, he would think about playing with his friend, the purple puppet, so he always looked forward to his next visit to Nana's house.

One Saturday morning Elliot's mom surprised him and told him and his older sister, Maddie, to get their jackets on because they were going to visit Nana, their great grandma, and her daughter who they referred to as Grandma. Elliot was so excited because he would get to visit his grandmas and play with the purple puppet once again.

When they arrived, Elliot gave his Nana and Grandma a great big hug. As they hugged, Elliot noticed a new art easel that Grandma bought with all the colorful markers and a big roll of drawing paper to color on. The easel even had two sides to it so he and Maddie both could draw at the same time.

So, while their mom was hanging up jackets and getting their baby sister out of her carrier seat, Elliot and Maddie started working on their next masterpieces of art.

Elliot drew a beautiful pink heart for his Nana and Maddie drew an elegant picture of a ballet dancer.

Before he was even finished with his picture, Elliot knew his next thing to play with would be the purple puppet. He gave his heart picture to Nana and quickly went to get the puppet off the hook before Maddie had a chance to get it.

He loved to make the puppet dance to music so he asked his grandma if she would play some music. Grandma turned on some music and away the two went, dancing down the hallway with the purple puppet keeping up with their steps.

13

Elliot felt like the puppet was ready to have a name. He wanted to pick just the right name, so he asked his grandma, "Would it be all right to name the purple puppet?"

Grandma replied, "Sure! Give it any name you want to. That one can be your puppet to play with."

Elliot thought for a few minutes and said, "I was thinking about naming him Gus," and then he hesitated, "but the only problem is, what if tomorrow Gus decides he doesn't want to be a boy anymore?"

Grandma was quick to reply, "Hold on just a minute, Elliot!"

Grandma continued, "That puppet is yours to name, and it will be what you say it is. It will not change its mind tomorrow because you are the one who gets to name it. You are the puppet's creator. It's the same way with God. He created you to be a little boy, so you'll always be a boy. You'll grow up one day to become a big boy, but you'll always be a boy because God creates us in His image. He knew that the best way to make you was to make you a boy. Sometimes we get frustrated and may wish to be someone else, sometimes we may even wish to be a cute little puppy, but we need to remember that God knew what was best for us the day he created us. He could have made you a little puppy, but he knew that you would have a better life as a boy.

So, if we ever get confused about what is best for us, just remember that God doesn't cause the confusion because He knew from the beginning what was best for you. And God doesn't make mistakes.

Let me explain a little more. Do you remember that heart you made for your Nana earlier today? You created that heart just for her to show her that you love her. What if I took that heart and colored on top of it and made it into a square or a circle. How would that make you feel?"

Elliot answered, "It would make me sad."

Grandma added, "That's how God feels when we try to change what He has created. It makes Him sad, too."

"Let me ask you something else," Grandma said. "Did you ever go fishing with your mom or dad?"

Elliot answered, "Yeah! I caught a fish, too!"

"Well, what did the fish do when you caught him with your fishing pole?"

Grandma's question got Elliot to thinking. "The fish wiggled all over the place! I think he was mad!" he replied.

Grandma explained, "That's because the fish wanted to be back in the water where God created him to be because that's where he is the most comfortable. What did you do with the fish after you caught him?"

Elliot answered, "We took him off the hook and put him back in the river. Dad said that he was just too small to keep."

21

Grandma asked, "What did the fish do when you put him *back* in the water? Did he seem happy or was he still mad?"

Elliot replied, "He was happy to be back in the water. He just swam away, and he was calm, not angry anymore."

"The reason he was calm is *that* is where his comfort zone was. The fish isn't sad, or scared, or angry if he's in the water. That's where God made him to be comfortable because He created him to be a fish. And He created you to be a boy.

So, *your* puppet will be named Gus and will be comfortable with that because *you* wanted him to be a boy." Grandma gave Elliot a hug and he seemed content with her explanation.

Elliot spent the rest of the visit with his new friend, Gus. He was glad that Gus now had a name, and he was happy that Gus was a puppet who could dance with him and walk with him. Somehow, that just made Elliot's world a little happier. And Gus seemed perfectly content, as well.

The End

Printed in the United States
by Baker & Taylor Publisher Services